THE MOST HILARIOUS, BIZARRE AND UNUSUAL CORRECTIONAL STORIES EVER TOLD

THE MOST HILARIOUS, BIZARRE AND UNUSUAL CORRECTIONAL STORIES EVER TOLD

DAN M. REYNOLDS

TOTAL
PUBLISHING
& MEDIA

Published by Total Publishing & Media
5411 South 125th East Ave.
Tulsa, Ok. 74146
www.totalpublishingand media.com

Published in the United States of America

ISBN: 978-1-63302-150-1
Biography & Autobiography / Criminals & Outlaws
14.10.09

I dedicate this book to all employees working in our correctional facilities, jails, and probation and parole districts. They do a great service for the people they serve.

Acknowledgments

I want to thank Ann Toyer and Debby Anderson for their expertise in assisting and editing the stories in the book. I also want to thank all those who provided stories for the book.

ACKNOWLEDGMENTS

Contents

Introduction

After working in corrections over thirty years and serving as a national correctional consultant, as well as a member of several correctional organizations, I have heard many hilarious, bizarre and unusual correctional stories. The stories contained in the book are based on true events, which have occurred in our prisons, jails, or probation and parole districts all across the United States. The stories may not be recent and some stories are well over forty years old. They may have been told on a number of occasions, but never published in a collection.

The stories may not all be hilarious, nor bizarre or unusual. A story may be hilarious to one and bizarre to another. A project manager for my publishing company put it well, "Although some stories can make people laugh, it brings up some ugly truth to the lighter side." It is not the intent of this author to poke fun, belittle, embarrass, or degrade any staff, inmate, or civilian by sharing these stories. Names of individuals, agencies, departments, facilities or states are not mentioned. When you have a group of individuals confined in a particular area with constant monitoring and supervision, things are going to happen—those things at times may be hilarious, bizarre, or unusual. The stories contained in this book are a sample of those events.

Grandma's Gone Wild!

A female correctional officer, who also happened to be a grandmother, took her job duties to another level. Correctional officers are responsible for monitoring and securing inmates who are incarcerated. However, grandma correctional officer added an additional job assignment to her job description and became sexually involved with a much younger inmate. This love affair apparently had been going on for months and intensified as time went on. Grandma correctional officer and this vulnerable young inmate would have sexual encounters on the desk in the chief of security's office, in the back of a pickup truck, in a nearby cemetery, or anytime their passions would arise. No place was off limits to these lovebirds.

One Saturday afternoon, the correctional officer noticed her inmate boyfriend visiting with a woman in the inmate visitation room. Enthralled by what she witnessed, she descended into a jealous rage, went to a nearby office, grabbed a pair of scissors, and was en-route to do some damage to her competition. Toting scissors in hand, she sprinted toward her lover. Other inmates took note of the situation, realizing grandma was heading toward the visitation room with the quickness of a feline chasing a mouse. They were able to stop her and wrestle the scissors from her hand, thus avoiding a potential fatal attraction episode with the unsuspecting two-timer.

Undeterred by the intervention, grandma wanted revenge. She would later solicit two inmates to help her take care of her cheating boyfriend. She offered to pay them $1,500 to do him in i.e., kill him. The inmates did not take her seriously at first but, later, found out she was dead serious and really wanted to have her boyfriend taken out. The inmates went to the boyfriend and warned him that his grandma girlfriend was attempting to put a contract out on his life. After a lengthy discussion and convincing the boyfriend the threat was genuine, they drew up a course of action to thwart her scheme. They plotted to get her contract to kill offer on tape, knowing that if they went to the authorities with hearsay information about a correctional officer, no one would believe an inmate. So they smuggled a tape recorder (as only inmates could) and got grandma on tape talking about the murder for hire plot. Then the inmates went to the authorities and handed over the taped conversation with grandma. The sheriff's office sent their deputies to the facility and placed grandma under arrest for conspiracy to commit murder. She went to court, pled guilty, and was placed on probation. She received a deferred sentence. She was also terminated from her job.

Preacher Cuts Inmate

A preacher's wife who was volunteering at a nearby prison got involved in an adulterous relationship with an inmate over a period of time. The wife, overcome with guilt and shame about the ongoing affair, finally broke the news to her husband one day while he was home for lunch. Once the wife told her husband about the affair, the preacher in a rage of anger got into his Cadillac and sought out the inmate.

The unsuspecting inmate was on a tractor, cutting grass in a field. The offended preacher raced his Cadillac across the prairie toward the tractor the inmate was riding. The preacher jumped out of his car, ran toward the inmate knife in hand. He then jumped up on the tractor and was able to slash the inmate's throat. Fearing for his life, the inmate fought off the preacher, knocking him to the ground. The inmate sped off in an effort to get away from the knife-wielding preacher. The preacher attempted to pursue the inmate via his Cadillac but got stuck and had to end the pursuit.

"What Do You Mean We Buried the Wrong Inmate?"

A warden at a maximum security facility was on vacation when he received a call around one thirty in the morning from one of his deputy wardens.

"Warden, I have some bad news." The warden's initial thought was that there had been a fight. "There was a funeral for our inmates who committed suicide. Now it has been discovered the wrong inmate was buried." Before the warden could catch himself, he made a few remarks to the deputy warden that he probably shouldn't have and, later, had to apologize for those comments made out of haste and anger. But he could not believe he had just learned he buried the wrong inmate.

The deputy warden continued to tell the story. Note that inmates are typically double celled in what is known as the receiving area. In this location, inmates have come from jails from all over the state and are processed into the Department of Corrections from this receiving area.

One inmate, who was assigned to a particular cell, had to have his cell location changed because he claimed he could not climb up the stairs due to a medical issue. Upon verifying that he did in fact have a medical issue and was prohibited from climbing stairs, the officer assigned him to another cell. He was then moved to a downstairs cell. However, the officer failed to make the cell change on the count sheet as was standard procedure. This procedure is completed to document and track the names of inmates and their assigned cells.

Two other inmates were assigned to the cell that this particular inmate had just vacated. Subsequently, one of those inmates left, leaving now only one inmate in the top cell. This lone inmate later committed suicide by hanging himself in the cell. Officers conducting a routine count discovered the lone inmate hanging in the cell and initiated CPR but to no avail. He was later pronounced dead at the hospital. When the hospital called the facility, wanting to know the name of the inmate, the officer went back, looked on the count sheet, and gave him the name of the inmate that had been assigned to that cell. Remember, the officer failed to update the count sheet when the inmate with the medical condition had moved downstairs. So this inmate's name was given to the hospital in error.

The officer gave hospital personnel the inmate's name and next of kin according to the records on file. The hospital then notified the family that their son has died. When the family reached the hospital in order to identify the body, the mother takes one look at the body and says that he is not her son. But the father disagrees and positively identifies the body as his son.

As protocol, the funeral home retrieves the body for burial. The family makes another trip to the funeral home, and again, the mother questions if the deceased is really her son. The mother is told he looks different because of the buzz haircut, embalming fluid, swelling etc.

Unbeknownst to all, is that the inmate with the medical condition who had vacated the top cell and the inmate who had committed suicide were around the same age, height, weight, and both had a buzz haircut. In the middle of this identification conversation is the funeral home that is relying on the family to make a positive identification of the deceased. But a wary mother still does not feel certain that the body they have is really her son. The undertaker proceeds with the funeral, and the inmate is buried.

That evening after the funeral and the grieving parents are at home, the phone rings. The voice on the other end says, "Dad, what are you doing?"

The dad responds, "I just got back from your funeral." The son had called his dad to ask him to send him money.

The dad said, "You can't be in prison. We just buried you!"

The son said, "I am not dead. I am at the prison."

The father calls the prison and speaks with the captain, explaining that his son just called him and his son tells him he is at the prison. The captain begins an attempt to find out what has really happened. He calls the unit to determine if the son is there and verifies his cell unit. Sure enough, the son is in fact alive and well. The correctional staff is able to retrace the course of events and figured out what had happened. They determine that the count sheet never got changed and the name given to the hospital was the wrong inmate.

The deputy warden is now convincing the warden what really happened via telephone. The warden gets out of bed and goes to the facility, where he finds both of his deputy wardens and the chief of security wrapping up the chain of events, which caused the mistaken identity crisis. Just to be sure, the warden verifies for himself that the inmate in the cell is in fact the one they thought they had just buried. He obtained a photo of the inmate who was buried, and sure enough, they looked very much alike.

Now the warden now has to call his boss to report what has happened. It is now around 6:00 a.m. The warden now has to call the family, a brother, of the inmate that is deceased and report his death and explain the entire mix up. The brother was not surprised to hear his brother had committed suicide because of a lengthy drug history starting at an early age. But when the warden told him he was already buried, the brother went ballistic, wanting to know how his brother could be buried prior to the family being notified. He then refused to continue the conversation and advised the correctional official that the next person they would be speaking to would be his attorney.

The warden now calls the family of the inmate who is alive. This revelation upsets the mother, and she demands that she be allowed to come to the prison and see her son in the flesh. She wanted to make sure he was okay and that this was not a joke being played on the family. She was allowed to visit her son, and after visiting her son, mother and daughter went to the warden's office. Rightfully so, the mother was livid and cursed the warden over the whole ordeal.

"I've never been yelled at like that before. There was nothing I could do but to listen and apologize," said the warden. The family positively identified the body and signed for him. The warden received permission to exhume the body for positive identification through fingerprints.

The brother of the buried inmate also would not be convinced his brother was deceased until fingerprints were taken. The brother had another funeral conducted and buried his brother in another city.

In a settlement with both families, the state agreed to pay all expenses related to the funeral. After the debacle was all over, the warden said it was one of the most difficult times in his career. Everyone seemed to alienate themselves from him and avoided him like the plague. He was needled from colleagues in and from other states saying, "Don't you know how to count inmates?" or "what kind of count system do you have?" He also received e-mails that read, "Warden Buries Wrong Inmate!"

After a lengthy and thorough investigation, it was concluded that an officer had failed to correct the count sheet. This officer was doing the work of three staff members. The department wanted to discipline this employee for the mix up, but the warden took a stand and refused to do so since the officer was so overwhelmed with the duties of three people.

In the aftermath of the incident, any inmate death requires the deceased to be fingerprinted and positively identified before burial. A system was implemented requiring a stand-up count where the officer would positively identify each offender with a photo ID once every twenty-four hours. The warden said, "You would never think you would be a part of such a bizarre incident during your career. It tested my leadership skills. That was the most bizarre thing that has ever happened to me, trumping the time an inmate died within a week of being given the wrong medication under my watch."

Three Hots and a Cot

An inmate who finally made his way down to minimum custody was now assigned to a community correctional center located right in the heart of a growing and bustling city. He was looking forward to tasting a little more freedom than what he had been use to in the past ten years or so. He was expected to begin preparing himself to make a successful reentry and reintegration back into society. He had to find a job within thirty days, save some money to pay off his courts cost, restitution, pay a deposit for an apartment plus have enough funds to turn on his utilities. After several weeks of job searching, he finally landed a job at a local hotel as a dishwasher in the kitchen. He worked Tuesday through Saturday from 10:00 a.m. to 6:00 p.m. He was fortunate enough to find a job within walking distance from the correctional center.

Each day, as he walked to work, he passed by several homeless people sleeping on the sidewalks and alleys. He got to the point where he began to recognize the people and would even make friendly gestures to them as he passed.

He met one homeless man that appeared to be about his age with similar physical characteristics. He was about the same height and weight, same eye, and hair color. He could have actually passed as his brother. The inmate had even started to stop and talk with this homeless man during his walk to work. These two men became pretty good friends as they started to become familiar with one another.

The inmate met a girl at the hotel where he was working. He found out she was also on probation and lived in a nearby apartment. They began to meet up on their breaks in undisclosed locations in order to spend more time with each other. He really liked her, and she liked him as well. So she gave him an open invitation to her place for drinks. The inmate was excited as to the potential of this relationship but did not know how he could pull it off. If he were not back at the center at a certain time, correctional officials would come looking for him. If they had to look for him, there would be the possibility that he would be sent back to higher security. After weeks of trying to figure out a way he could go see his girlfriend, he came up with a plan. The plan involved his homeless friend. If he could get the homeless man to check in the center as himself, he would have the advantages and benefits of three meals a day and a warm place to stay, especially during those cold and bitter winter nights. He would just need the homeless man to check himself out each day as if he was going to work.

The inmate finally approached the homeless man with his idea, and after a short deliberation, the homeless man agreed to the plan. The inmate gave the homeless man his facility identification card, which would be needed to check in and out of the center. The inmate told him what to expect from other inmates and staff at the center, including the proper responses to questions that staff may ask of him. The inmate even drew a map of the interior of the facility so he would know his way around the center, where his assigned bunk was, the names of his bunkmates, and especially where the kitchen was since that is where he was going to get his meals.

Now everything was set up so he could spend an evening with his girlfriend at her place. The inmate was looking forward to spending time with a woman since he had not been with one for a long, long time. Well, this arrangement proved to be successful for several weeks until the homeless man failed to show up one evening at the center. The homeless man was listed as an escapee from custody. Staff and local law enforcement were notified, and a search took place to find the escaped inmate. The inmate was later arrested and apprehended as he showed up to work at the hotel. He was later sent back to prison to do the remainder of his time. It would be interesting to know if the inmate felt what he did was worth a return to prison!

Get Your Free Turkey from Personnel

A correctional officer walked into his supervisor's office one day engulfed in uncontrollable laughter. After gaining his composure, he began to tell his boss what was so amusing.

He said, "You know that new female employee that recently started?"

The boss nods his head in the affirmative. "Well, the training officer cannot stand her and really has it in for her. So during one of their chance encounters, he asked if she had been to personnel to get her free thanksgiving turkey. She responded that she had not. The training officer informed her that during the Thanksgiving holiday season, the prison gives each employee a turkey to take home to his or her family. Hearing this, the female employee became so excited regarding the prison's generosity that she immediately heads to the personnel department to retrieve her free turkey."

The mischievous training officer, keeping his distance but following the female employee to the personnel office, watched as she announced to the personnel officer that she was there to pick up a free turkey. The personnel officer is fairly new, and is still learning the ins and outs of his new job duties looked puzzled and said, "What free turkey?"

The female employee went on to explain that during the Thanksgiving holidays, employees are told to come to the personnel office to get a free turkey. The personnel officer said, "Well, I don't have any turkeys, plus no one has mentioned that I am suppose to give out free turkeys, but I will call to find out what is going on?"

The female employee waited patiently while the personnel director tried to call his supervisor and then other department heads to determine what he was supposed to do about the "free turkey" giveaway. The waiting female employee grew more and more impatient about the turkey and was now starting to demand her turkey be given to her now. The personnel director apologized to her and said he was doing all he could to find out more about the free turkey giveaway. He was unsure if he was to pass turkeys out or not. Why he didn't even know where the turkeys were kept even if he was to pass them out.

The female employee now really fuming with anger and began to slam her fist on the counter and said, "Hurry-up. I can't wait all day. Where is my turkey?" The personnel director, unable to reach any authority figure, was becoming more and more frustrated and rattled because he did not know how to handle the enraged female employee. Finally, she left in disgust and anger. So now both she and the dubious personnel director were totally emotional angered and drained from their contentious meeting that had just taken place.

The naughty training officer taking in the entire scene from a safe distance was laughing so hard he fell to his knees as the tears streamed down his face.

The Criminal Prayer

An infamous inmate who had a reputation for filing and winning lawsuits against a particular state admitted he believed in God and even prayed before he committed his specialized trade that he had perfected—home burglaries. He prayed to God for his safety and that no one would get hurt. He trusted God would watch after him during his time of sin and evildoings.

Ghosts at Warden's Mansion

Ghost at the warden's house located on the grounds of the state penitentiary? Yes!

Where would one start to recount the many poltergeist experiences? Why even some could share a few unbelievable ghost encounters. Below are some scary examples:

Those Unexplained Touches. Once I stood in the middle of the white room and felt someone or something brush up against my back or the time a hand lay on my back while I brushed my teeth as if to make sure my daily good habits were taking place.

Coughing Sound and Footsteps. How about the cough and the feel of someone sinking down on the edge of the twin bed where I slept or the faint sounds of footsteps that whispered over the wood floor? Some were pretty intense.

Voices. My friend heard people talking in my bedroom. Or the time I heard my name called a few times, and my pet cockatiel would go nuts in his birdcage when no inhabited body was near.

Strange Occurrences in the Basement. Yes, the eerie basement. I used to love playing pool in the basement all by myself until the creepiest thing happened. I had a few girlfriends over for the weekend, and we wanted to play some pool. While we walked down the narrow plush carpeted staircase, the barroom door slammed in our faces. My mother said it sounded like a herd of elephants trampled up the stairs and a slew of monkeys screaming. With white faces and pounding hearts, I slammed the door to the basement that day and swore never to return by myself again. And never did I go back to that basement by myself. I kept my promise.

A Credit Card Scam

A bright, intelligent inmate with an above average IQ was able to get people from the outside to obtain credit card numbers. He had a girlfriend who worked at a convenience store. He was able to get her to give him credit card numbers and their expiration dates. He would then charge expensive items on those credit cards and have the merchandise delivered to the residence of several staff members. Some of those hot items included riding lawn mowers, delivery of flowers to female staff, and even electronics. He only wished he could see the look on the faces of those employees when their merchandise arrived on their doorstep.

Corrections Staff
Solicit Inmate's Advice

One day in the month of April, a staff member observed a large number of other staff members lined up in front of the cell of a well-known and notorious inmate. With some investigation and questioning, it was learned the inmate who was considered to be a very bright, educated, and intelligent was offering staff tax advice on how to save money on their tax returns.

I Escaped Because I Would Miss My Scheduled Hip Surgery!

An inmate in his 50s was within three weeks of being released from a minimum security prison when he suddenly walked away from the nonbarrier facility where he was staying. When he was captured a few hours later, he was asked, "Why would you run-off when you are so close of being discharged."

The inmate stated, "I have been locked up for twenty-five years. Society has nothing to offer me, and I don't have anything to offer society. And besides, I have hip surgery scheduled in a few months, and if I discharge my sentence now, I would not be able to get my hip fixed. I don't have any money or insurance to pay for the surgery. This is my home."

Police Refused
to Go into Neighborhood

Two inmates walked away from a minimum security facility late one evening. After extensive intelligence gathered and chased down leads, information was received regarding the whereabouts of the escapees. The location was in a small town near the border of an adjoining state. When the correctional officers located the house they believed the inmates were taking refuge, they contacted the local police for assistance. When the correctional officers gave the location of the house, to their dismay, the police refused to go into the crime-ridden neighborhood.

The police, fearing for their own safety, had refused to cooperate and assist the correctional officers in capturing the fugitives. Knowing they couldn't go back to the facility empty-handed, the correctional officers were able to successfully slip into the neighborhood undetected and apprehend the escapees, returning them to the facility without incident.

Probation and Parole Officer Shoots the Local Town's Mayor

A probation and parole officer who frequented a well-known restaurant in the local town was having lunch with a friend of his who just happened to be the town's mayor. Before they were able to leave the restaurant, the mayor was shot in the leg by his probation and parole officer friend. It was later revealed that the officer's wife had placed a small handgun in his pants that morning. The officer, who forgot the gun was in his pants, reached in his pocket to retrieve some change to pay for the meal and accidentally discharged the weapon. The bullet shot a hole in the officer's pants pocket, traveled under the table, and lodged in the mayor's leg. The mayor was taken to the town's local hospital to remove the bullet from his leg.

Fleeing Felon Unknowingly Runs into a Correctional Facility

At two thirty on a September morning, a lieutenant at a correctional facility was conducting a routine foot patrol on the facility grounds. He heard a sound just outside the fence line to the south of the facility, which sounded like a vehicle accident. The lieutenant began running toward the front gate to see if he could offer any assistance or provide emergency services to anyone, if there was an injury. He radioed another officer, who was at the security control office, to open the front gate. As the lieutenant was running through the front gate, an unidentified black male, approximately six feet or taller wearing black pants and a T-shirt ran past him, shouting, "There has been a bad wreck back there."

The lieutenant shouted at the unidentified male several times to stop, but he refused to comply with the lieutenant's verbal order. The lieutenant then chased him through the facility compound when suddenly, the man quickly climbed over the fence. The lieutenant quickly ran back to the security control office and notified metropolitan police.

The man, who was actually a fleeing felon, had lost control of his vehicle and ran head-on into a light pole. He then got out of his wrecked vehicle and ran unknowingly through a nearby community correctional center right into the path of the lieutenant. The suspect ran to the corner of the compound and crawled over an eight foot security fence. It is unknown if the man was ever apprehended by police.

Inmate Breaks Up a Fight Between Staff Members

Two correctional officers were in a heated argument, which later escalated into a shoving match. The confrontation was broken up by an inmate who happened to be in the area and witnessed the altercation. The officers were later severely disciplined. The inmate walked away scratching his head at what had just transpired.

Sex Ring at a Women's Prison

A sex-ring operation, which had been in existence for some time, was in full operation on a particular midnight shift at a female prison. A certain number of staff involved in this enterprise had devised a scheme to get sex plus make money on the side. Staff became pimps behind bars for the women. Anyone who was willing to pay for sex could do so with these experienced felons. The female inmates would take a portion of the money while the pimps took in profits. An investigation was initiated once a complaint was lodged against a staff member for sexual assault. As the investigation grew larger, it was discovered that the sex ring involved a sizeable number of inmates and staff.

Miss Inmate Beauty Pageant

Miss Inmate Beauty Pageant in the 1980s consisted of a modeling and talent contest at the state's maximum security facility for women. The contestants compete with other female inmates by displaying personality, intelligence, talent skills, clothing, and the most notable criteria, the catwalk. It was like an abridged prison version of *Project Runway*.

The inmate contestants were allowed to showcase their talents for the judges. One inmate showcased her talents with roller-skating. The winner of the contest received the title of Miss Inmate and as an added bonus, the warden crowned the winner, kissed her on the cheek and escorted her around the facility—a big self-esteem booster to the lucky lady.

Glad to Be at Home

As inmates were being received in the state's maximum security prison, a twenty-two-year-old clean-cut, blond hair, and blue-eyed inmate proclaimed to a staff member, "I am glad to be home."

The officer, confused and curious as to the strange comment made by the young inmate, finally asked him, "What do you mean you are glad to home?"

To that question, the inmate explained that twenty-two years ago, his father was an inmate here and his mother was incarcerated at the nearby women's prison. This young lad said he was conceived at the prison.

I Will Kill Myself Before You Can Kill Me !

An inmate who was within twenty-four hours of his execution was able to get his hands on enough pills to cause his overdose and possibly die before the state could execute him. Prison officials transported him to a local hospital to have his stomach pumped and later returned him in time for his scheduled execution, which was successfully carried out.

But I Had to Go Pee!

A correctional division officer was unable to hire full time staff and decided to reach out and solicit assistance from a community resource. The office was in need of a temporary receptionist position. The personnel agency sent over a gentleman, who was in his seventies, to monitor the front desk. His duties included answering the telephone and greeting visitors. When the elderly gentleman suddenly had to use the restroom, his timing couldn't have been worse. His urgency occurred during lunch hour, and office staff had left for lunch. To avoid abandoning the front desk, he decided his only option was to urinate in a Coke bottle. Being upset that he had to urinate in a bottle instead of going to the restroom, he decided to give the Coke bottle filled with his urine to his supervisor who in turn gave it to her supervisor. The man was later terminated. He said he felt like he could not abandon his newly assigned post.

A Sexual Electrocution

A call came in at central control with information about an inmate who was discovered dead in an electrical chase. Upon arriving at the scene, correctional staff observed an inmate lying on his back totally nude. After closer observation, the inmate had live electrical electrodes attached to his testicles. Pornographic pictures were found near his body. Apparently, the inmate had a practice of getting into the electrical chase when staff was preoccupied and hooking himself up to electrodes for sexual gratification as he was engrossed over pornographic pictures.

A Creative Method for Obtaining a Clean Urine Test

A staff member was conducting a routine shakedown of an inmate's bunk when he found a series of plastic tubing. The staff member inquired and questioned the inmate regarding the purpose of the plastic tubing and why it was in his possession. After further questioning and probing the inmate, he finally admitted he was using it to get a clean urine test. The inmate explained that one end of the tube was inserted in his penis and the other end was placed inside another inmate's penis. The willing participant would urinate through the plastic tube and dump clean urine into the other inmate's bladder, which caused him to have a clean urine test at the scheduled time.

My Last Meal

As is routine for the fate of an inmate facing execution, the male or female is asked what he or she would like for their last meal. For one particular execution the inmate replied that all he wanted for his last meal was a rabbit. The warden was not sure how or if he could comply with the inmates last wishes but decided to consult with his staff. One staff member took on the challenge and said he could find him a rabbit. So the following weekend, the staff member went rabbit hunting and was accosted by a game warden. This was not rabbit season. The game warden arrested the Good Samaritan for hunting rabbit out of season. The staff member was taken to jail and had to call the warden who eventually posted his bail so that he could be released from jail. The warden did keep his word, and the inmate did receive rabbit for his last meal.

A Tour of the
Prison Kitchen

The American Correctional Association (ACA) is responsible for ensuring that correctional agencies operate in compliance with national standards. Correctional agencies participate in an accreditation process on a continuous basis.

During an ACA reaccreditation audit of a maximum security facility, the ACA audit team was touring a facility kitchen and dining area. The ACA chairperson typically asks operational questions from the food service staff when touring an area where meals are served. At this particular food service area, a gentleman began explaining all the operations of the kitchen even quoting policy and procedure during the process.

The chairperson was extremely impressed with the cleanliness of the kitchen area and was satisfied with all the answers to the questions she had received. Near the end of the tour, the chairperson asked what was behind a closed door. The gentleman opened the door, and the audit team observed a bunk, mattress, linen, blanket, and a pillow.

The gentleman explained that was his bunk area. It finally occurred to the chairperson that the gentleman with all of the answers was an inmate and not staff. The inmate was allowed to have his quarters in the kitchen area. The inmate was so convincing the entire team believed the inmate was a staff member.

The Missing Leg

An elderly inmate was being held at the local hospital due to his advanced state of diabetes. One leg had already been amputated due to his diabetes. Finally, the inmate succumbed to the disease.

The prison was notified by the hospital that the inmate had expired, and hospital officials requested that someone from the facility come and retrieve the body. Since the inmate had no family who could ensure the body would be transported to a funeral home for regular burial services, two officers were sent to the hospital with a body bag to retrieve the deceased.

The officers traveled to the hospital in the wintry weather, which was cold and rainy, along icy roads. The officers were directed by hospital personnel to go to the hospital morgue and pick up the inmate. Upon arriving at the morgue, they noticed that a leg in a plastic bag had been placed near the inmate's body. The officers assumed the leg belonged to the inmate, so they took the leg along with the body back to the prison. When the officers returned the inmate to the institution, he was placed in a standard casket with the leg and was transported to the prison cemetery. The chaplain held a brief service, and the grave was filled.

Within an hour, the institution received a telephone call from the hospital wanting to know if the officers had picked up an "extra leg" when they picked up the inmate's body. When it was determined that they had, the hospital requested that the leg be returned so tests could be run on the extremity.

Considering that the grave had been covered and a court order would be necessary to open the grave, the district attorney's office was consulted. Upon being told that the grave had just been closed, they were advised to go ahead and open the grave and retrieve the leg. The officers retraced their burial steps aided with heavy equipment and shovels. The grave was recovered, and the leg placed in its plastic bag was transported to the hospital. Needless to say, this entire incident was kept under the radar and did not make the local newspapers. Very little information outside of required internal documentation regarding this incident left the agency.

Bomb Threat at the State Capital

A bomb threat was received at the state capital during a legislative session. The capital police taking the threat seriously, evacuated all persons in the building. After an investigation, it was learned an inmate assigned to administrative segregation in a maximum security prison was able to telephone the state capital and call in the bomb threat. Thankfully, no injuries were reported; however, the warden from the facility where the call came from had some serious explaining to do. The inmate found himself confined to a customized cell with special security features to prevent limited contact with staff, other inmates, as well as the public.

A Letter to the Warden

It is not unusual for inmates to write the warden of their facility requesting action or for information. One prison warden received a very unusual letter from one of his inmates. The inmate wrote that he had heard from other inmates about a new program that would allow you to receive up to 500 days off your sentence, if the inmate would agree to full castration. The inmate said he has been struggling with the decision for weeks and even months and had decided that 500 days was worth losing his family jewels and gaining his freedom. The warden finally had to break the bad news to the inmate and tell him there was no such program at the prison.

Apprehension by the Finger Gun

One late evening, as an inmate was running from the correctional facility attempting to escape, a quick-thinking officer yelled at the inmate to stop. The inmate continued to run to avoid being captured. The officer yelled again for the inmate to stop, but to no avail. The officer yelled a third time to stop, but also said, "Stop, or I will shoot."

The inmate looked back at the officer and saw the officer's arms and hands extended out, and it appeared he had a weapon in his hand, so the inmate stopped. The officer ordered the inmate to get on the ground, face down with his hands behind his head. As the officer approached, he continued extending his arms and hands until he was close enough to put cuffs on the inmate. The officer never had a gun or any other type weapon in his hand, but the inmate didn't know it. The officer had his right index finger extended with his right thumb sticking up making it appear that he had a gun.

Homicide in Blood Alley

Prisoners had to be particularly aware during their walk through Blood Alley. Blood Alley was space between the Garment Factory and the Mess Hall. Many of men have been stabbed, beaten, and strangled in this area. One day, a 170 pound inmate stuck another inmate in the chest until he fell on his back. The perpetrator continued to stab him multiple times until he could no longer pull the knife out of his chest cavity. Once guards were alerted and arrived on the scene, witnesses saw an officer unable to pull the knife out of the inmate's chest, after numerous attempts. Finally, to do so, he had to put one foot on his chest for leverage in order to successful remove the knife from the 230 pound dead inmate's chest.

Lost in Translation

In the late 1990s, an inexperienced community corrections classification officer got away with one. The local city court referred a client to the local reentry center. The individual was ordered to serve four days on a misdemeanor Driving Under Suspension charge. This individual was not only far from home during this ordeal, but he also did not speak or understand English.

Based on the client's physical appearance, the classification officer assumed the client was male. He also could not make sense of the client's written name to make a gender determination. Somehow intake staff had failed to review identification at processing. So the client was placed in a sleeping room designated for males.

For four days, the client resided in the male sleeping room. Maybe because of cultural differences or just not wanting to rock the boat, this person never complained or reported a concern. For the next four days, staff and clients alike had no clue this person was actually a woman. At the client's exit from the facility, the person's gender finally became known.

The classification officer turned green when he learned of his error. After saying a few prayers, the officer telephoned his boss to report the snafu. His prayers were answered as his boss thought it was funny. A lesson learned—never judge a book by its cover.

Locked Up in Maximum Security

During a correctional conference, tours were being provided to a nearby maximum security prison for the conference participants. A group of correctional professionals boarded a bus and were taken to the prison; checked in, searched, and the tour began.

During the tour, as the group was leaving an administrative segregation unit, they entered a long hallway. An officer was posted at each entrance and exit of the hallway. As the group went down the hall and approached the door leading out of the hallway, the deputy wardens who were leading the tour were unable to get the officer's attention to open the door to let them out. The deputy wardens banged on the door for several minutes, to no avail. After fifteen to twenty minutes, one of the deputy wardens took off his shoe and used the bottom of his shoe to bang on the door, attempting to get the officer's attention. One of the deputy wardens laughed and said it should not be this hard to get out of here since a few years ago, some inmates were able to escape out of this same hallway. Some of the tour participants responded with a nervous laugh.

Finally, after approximately forty-five minutes, one officer finally discovered that there were people in the hallway and popped open the door. It was later learned that the proper protocol was for the assigned correctional officer to use a hand-held walkie-talkie and notify the officer stationed at the other end of the hallway when people were in the hallway. The officer would then open the door to let them exit the hallway. In this particular case, the tour group entered and the officer that let them in left during shift change and failed to notify the other officer assigned to the other end of the hallway that people were in the hallway. The oncoming officer had no knowledge people were in the hallway since there was no cameras or communication devices to alert the officer. Needless to say, all participants taking the tour were relieved when that door finally popped open!

The Scent That Chased Off a Skunk

A large medium security facility was in the path of a hurricane's destruction. The terror in the air caused major flooding and power outages. The facility was forced to evacuate immediately. Some inmates had to be rescued by boat. Many first responders were not able to reached the inmates and staff for days on end.

Staff and inmates went without food, water, and clothing and hygiene items. Finally, after several days, all the stranded inmates and staff were rescued, and everyone's life was spared. After all the inmates and staff were accounted for, they were transported to other correctional facilities in the state, which extended late in the evening.

As inmates were stripping off their wet-and-soiled clothing, they threw them in the back of a pickup truck in a secluded wooded area. The scent from the soiled clothing had a disgusting and nauseating odor that was almost more than anyone could bear. Suddenly, a skunk was observed coming out of the thick brush and was headed right toward the truck. As the skunk got near enough to the disgusting scent eluding from the clothes, it turned away and ran back into the woods.

Generation Gap

A Prime Example

A tenured correctional supervisor was providing employee orientation to some new recruits. The supervisor was going over the dress code and what was acceptable attire for employees to wear in the workplace. As the supervisor was reading down his list of unacceptable attire, he mentioned that no thongs are allowed.

A young female in the back of the room with a puzzled and disturbed look on her face raised her hand with a question for the supervisor. When the supervisor called on her to ask her question, she said, "How are you going to know if I am wearing a thong or not?"

A Ghost in the Cemetery

A manhunt was underway to capture a presumed "armed and dangerous" convict who had escaped from his maximum security facility. Dozens of correctional personnel, along with local and state law enforcement officials, joined the search of the dangerous inmate. Track dogs were released to help pick up a scent and locate a direction of travel.

Hours passed without a trace of the escaping convict. Suddenly, as nightfall appeared and all was pitch-dark, the dogs located a scent, and officers discovered shoe tracks believed to belong to the escaping convict. The prints were fairly close together as if he was tired, lost, and possibly confused. The tracks led into an old cemetery, and the officers noticed the footprints became longer in scope as if the convict became to run through the cemetery.

As officers began to set up a perimeter around the cemetery to catch the convict, the officers were skeptical and were not so willing to go wandering through the cemetery at night. One creative officer got in his vehicle and got on the loud speaker and one could hear, "*Ooo... ooo...oooo...ooooo.*"

After several minutes, you could hear a voice deep imbedded in the dark cemetery. "Help! Help me! Here I am, over here, come get me!" The convict was apprehended without incident, and that story I would assume has been told several hundred times.

Who Can Break an Egg Between Their Legs with a Spoon?

During a hot August afternoon, the yard officer approached a group of inmates sitting under an old shade tree, looking for some good ole casual conversation. After a few minutes of chit-chat, the officer said, "You know it is impossible to break an egg with a spoon between your legs. It cannot be done."

The officer continues to say, "I've tried it, and it cannot be done. It sounds easy enough, but for some reason, it cannot be done."

After a lengthy debate, one inmate, by the nick-name of Van raised his hand, and said, "I can do it if anyone can!" The officer swore it could not be done by anyone. The inmate insisted he could do it, so they scrambled around and found a spoon and an egg for the ultimate test.

The inmate took the egg and placed it precisely between his legs, making sure it was real secure, and centered. When the inmate was ready, he took the handle of the spoon and took some practice swings to make sure to hit the egg dead center. As the others grew impatient, they began to chant, "Van, Van, he's our man. If he can't do it, no one can. Van, Van, he's our man, if he can't do it, no one can."

As Van slowly raised his hand with spoon tightly gripped in the palm of his hand, he paused with spoon in midair and, suddenly with a grueling blow, made contact with the egg, dead centered, and it sounded like a grenade going off. As Van opened his eyes, he became very still and motionless, you could hear a pin drop. The shattered egg particles, to include the yellow yoke covered his crouch area from side to side. After the cautious silence, laughter broke out for hours that unforgettable day. Van proved 'em wrong, you could break an egg with a spoon between your legs!

I Had to Confess When My Cell Partner Began to Stink

During an altercation between two cell partners the argument became violent and eventually deadly. It was a fight for life or death. After a bloody and vicious round of blows, kicks, and bites, one inmate lay dead in his cell.

The perpetrator quickly went into action to rid of any evidence of murder. After several hours of cleaning and disposing of any evidence of the fight, the perpetrator laid down on his bunk to rest and figure out what his next move would be, so he pondered. But he knew he could not ponder long because the correctional officer would be coming around making his count and ensuring all inmates were alive and well. The perpetrator had to act fast, so he put his dead cell partner in his bed and covered him with a sheet. He left only the top of his head showing with a small piece of flesh showing. He put a fan blowing in his cell partner's direction, which caused continuous movement of the sheet. He also rigged up a series of strings, one attached to his cell partner's leg, and the other attached to his arm.

As the officer would come by to count, he would tug on the string, making either his leg or arm move. Once the officer was convinced the inmate was alive and well and he saw flesh and movement, he went on to the next cell. This continued for three days until his cell partner began to stink, and the perpetrator could not stand the stench in the air any longer. He finally got the attention of an officer and told him to get his dead cell partner out of his cell. He couldn't stand the smell any longer. The perpetrator was later found guilty of murder and was sentenced to death.

When Your Blocker Retreats

Two correctional administrators were walking down a long-and-narrow hallway of a women's prison when out of nowhere, an inmate screamed out one of the men's name. She was a robust lady, and her scream filled the hallway.

While excitingly calling the administrator's name, she was also running toward him in what looked like a movie scene where long lost friends see each other from a distance and are running toward each other to embrace. The closer the inmate came, the larger the inmate appeared, and the sooner the other administrator realized that the hallway that they were standing in would not be large enough for the three of them once the inmate reached them. In a moment of survival thinking mode, the administrator, who also happened to be the smaller of the two, darted behind his colleague just in the nick of time before the full-bodied inmate made contact with her former supervisor.

The smaller administrator said, "If she ever made contact with me, I would have been a goner! She would have crushed me!"

Big Moma

Every now and then in a prison facility, inmates have to be extracted from their cell. Some would put up a fight, but no fight was as colorful as when a certain female inmate, Big Moma had to be extracted from her cell. Big Moma would prepare for her defensive battle. Her first line of defense was to rub herself in baby oil from head to toe and taunted staff to try and grab a hold of a large slippery female inmate. Then she would wrap magazines around her arms for when she had to use her karate blocking skills to obstruct any blows from the officers when they used their PR 24's (a wooden baton).

When the fight, or the technical term "cell extraction" would begin, a brave officer would go in and try to peacefully talk Big Moma out of her cell. This was not just any ordinary inmate. Big Moma had a reputation of whipping up on staff, male or female. The new officer of less than a year was designated to go in and talk with her and get her to come out of her cell peacefully and without force.

As the officer entered, staff outside the cell could hear one heck of a commotion, and suddenly, the officer's helmet came flying out of the cell followed by his baton moments later, and finally, he was seen running out of her cell. It was then time to call in the emergency squad for a cell extraction. Before the advent of sophisticated equipment for cell extractions were available, officers would use a mattress as a shield. They would use the mattress to force their way into the cell and protect against contact from the inmate.

When the second line of officers was forced to retreat, the big gun was brought in, the chief of security. The chief and his squad were finally able to subdue Big Moma and extract her out of her cell.

A New Cook in the Kitchen!

Each week, as had been a long standing tradition, staff from the various prison industries would have lunch on the women's ward. One day at lunch, a gentleman noticed his food just didn't taste right. Another gentleman at the same table also agreed that something just was not right with the food, but he could not put a finger on the problem.

Before you knew it, everyone was in agreement that the food had a peculiar and unfamiliar taste. The food service supervisor was immediately made aware of their concerns about the quality of food being served. They strongly suggested to the supervisor a need to inspect the preparation of the food was in order to establish a cause for the odd taste.

Taking their advice, the food service supervisor first reviewed the file of the recently hired cook and made a stunning discovery! The novice cook was doing time for poisoning two of her previous husbands. Needless to say, she was reassigned out of the kitchen for the protection of all.

How Are the Inmates Getting Drunk?

Several inmates in a particular cell block were discovered to be under the influence of intoxicating substances. In an effort to find their stash, a facility lockdown was ordered so correctional officers could do a thorough search. The search was found to be productive, and several gallons of homemade brew were confiscated.

A decision was made to keep the cell block locked down through the weekend. As staff returned to work the following Monday, they found it odd that the inmates were still acting as if they were under the influence. So once again, another facility shakedown was orchestrated and carried out, but this time, a more thorough search was conducted.

This included not only every cell but also offices, closets, and utility chases. After an exhausting search, an officer dismantled a utility chase door and discovered a fully operating still. After interviewing several inmates, it was discovered that a skilled plumber who had access to the cell block utility chases had built a still in one of the chases and had manufactured copper lines, which ran to individual cells.

Paying inmates were able to access the spirits while in their cell. If an inmate could not pay or did not pay on time, the plumber would simply shut off the spirits to occupants of that particular cell. The paying inmates had access to homemade spirits twenty-four hours a day, seven days a week.

Easy Money

A group of inmates in a maximum security prison, along with the assistance of a prison employee, devised a clever counterfeiting moneymaking scheme. Inmates who worked in the print shop were skilled in operating complex printing presses and its various components. They decided to use their prized skills to duplicate currency on the printing presses. They were able to carry out this scheme by obtaining either original or very similar paper used by the Department of Treasury to create sheets of counterfeit bills. When the sheets of bills were printed in the facility print shop, the inmates would intricately cut and properly size the sheets of paper currency.

The employee, who looked the other away as the inmate counterfeit operation continued, received a percentage of the money printed by the inmates. The inmates, along with the prison employee, would smuggle the currency out of the facility to awaiting family members. Once the phony currency were received by family members, it was converted into money orders or cashier's checks and then mailed back into the facility addressed to specific inmates. The inmates used the money to buy groceries from the prison store, which also included television sets, appliances, and other items.

People Who Live in Glass Houses

Everyone remembers Barney Fife, the overzealous deputy cop who could make a mountain out of a molehill in any situation. There was an officer in a community corrections facility that was known as the Barney Fife of their facility. He could find drugs or alcohol on anybody or anywhere and would go through great lengths to get the offender.

One time, he climbed on top of a roof to spy on suspects, and when the inmates got wind of his detective-like antics, they moved the ladder so that he could not get down from his post. Another time, he hid in a laundry cart, hoping to listen to inmate's conversations. Again when the inmates got wind of what he was doing, someone pushed the laundry cart down the hill with the snooping officer in it. But the chickens came home to roost episode was when the officer was transporting some inmates, and alcohol was detected. The tables were turned when the inmates revealed that the officer was the culprit and not them who reeked of alcohol.

You Can't Get Pregnant Standing Up?

———————

At a parole board meeting at a maximum security prison, an inmate was appearing from a community corrections center. The inmate appeared and left the room, and his girlfriend was there to testify in his behalf.

His girlfriend was about eight months pregnant. One of the parole board members, who enjoyed questioning the inmate's witnesses, asked her how she was pregnant because her boyfriend had been incarcerated for about two years. She stated that her and her boyfriend had sex in the restroom at the correctional center. She did this in a very apologetic manner and hastily added, "My boyfriend told me if we did it standing up, I wouldn't get pregnant."

The parole board members were falling out of their chairs laughing as everyone in attendance. After about three or four minutes, order was restored. A vote was taken, and the inmate was recommended for parole overwhelmingly. The inmate's girlfriend was tearfully overjoyed!

Help! I'm Being Chased by a Large Chicken!

A medium security inmate escaped from his secure confinement, and without a plan or knowing where he was going, other than getting as far away from the prison as he could, he began to run in the rural area through farmers fields and wooded acreage. After several hours of running, he came across a clearing that was fenced with chain link. Being tired and worn out from all the running and without food or water, he decided to take the easiest path, and that was climbing over the fence.

He managed to pull himself over the fence to the other side, which to him seemed like heaven, because he didn't have to maneuver through thick woods and underbrush only to be eaten up by the ticks, chiggers, and mosquitoes. As he was taken his sweet time making distance between himself and the prison, he heard a disturbing sound behind him. The sound seemed like something was snorting or growling at him. The sound grew louder as he heard something in the nearby woods getting closer to him. He began to run a little faster not knowing what was behind him.

As he was running, he heard the snorting again, and when he turned around, he saw an animal he never saw before, but it looked like a giant chicken. At this time, he began running for his life, and the giant chicken was fast approaching. Suddenly, he started screaming, "HELP! HELP! HELP ME!" He finally got the attention of a farmer tending to his crops. The farmer said what's wrong, and the escapee said, "A GIANT CHICKEN IS AFTER ME!" As the farmer turned and looked to see what was chasing the escapee, he noticed his pet emu seeking the escapee's attention. An emu is a large Australian bird resembling an ostrich but smaller. Emus cannot fly, but they can run very fast.

Gunshots Ring Out on Prison Grounds

A fairly new female correctional officer who was assigned to community corrections was tasked to assist in transporting an offender to a medium security facility. This was her first time to transport an inmate to a higher security prison.

As their van approached the perimeter of the prison, she exited the van to surrender her weapon. Since this was her first time to go through the process, she was a bit unsure what she was suppose to be doing, but she did know she was to clear her weapon by using the nearby clearing barrel located outside the fence as a big sign said, "Empty Weapon Here." As she approached the clearing barrel, she pointed her weapon inside the barrel and began firing her weapon until all six rounds were shot.

As nearby administrative and line personnel heard loud gunshots, they instinctively went to emergency mode and fell to the floor. Some staff began running out of buildings believing they were under attack. Men and women screamed and hollered for help. Once the dust settled, it was learned the officer thought to clear her weapon meant for her to fire all her bullets into the barrel rather than using the barrel to safely unload the rounds from the gun. She caused a stir that day. Needless to say, she was not invited back to the facility.

A High School Acquaintance?

Many who read this story will certainly relate to it because it has probably happen to you sometime during your career with corrections.

A twenty-year correctional employee walked into a busy restaurant for an early morning breakfast. As he sat and waited for his breakfast to arrive, a gentleman walked in. The employee recognized this gentleman as knowing him, but can't remember where. The gentleman also made eye contact with the employee and made a friendly wave in his direction and seemed glad to see him.

The gentleman approached the employee and screamed out his first and last name as he approached the table. He slapped the employee on the back and treated him like a long-lost friend. The gentleman asked the employee how he was getting along, and he wanted to get caught up on all years past. The employee believed the gentleman must have attended high school with him. Yeah, that was where he knew him—from high school. After the employee told the gentleman about his family, his children, his neighborhood, his new vehicle and current and distant relatives, as well as all the issues at work, the employee finally realized where he knew the gentleman from; it was not high school but a former prison he had worked at. The gentleman was an inmate who had been on the employee's correctional caseload when he was a case manager. Luckily for the employee, the inmate liked and respected the employee.

A County Jail Beauty!

A seasoned correctional employee was tasked going out of state to tour a county jail in hopes to secure a lease agreement to house overcrowded inmates for his particular state agency. As the employee was being escorted around the county jail and visiting various tiers of the jail, the employee turned the corner, and on the other side of the tier in the first cell on the right, he noticed the most beautiful woman he had ever laid eyes on.

She had all the curves and long hair, and her face was marked with just the right makeup to look fantastic. The employee turned and asked the jail administrator, "Oh, you house females as well?"

The jail administrator just looked at the employee and smiled and walked off. The employee knew right then that he had been had; that beautiful female offender was actually a male inmate who was posing as a female! The employee exclaimed, "But that was the most beautiful woman I have ever seen!"

Rocket Man

Inmates in years past have come up with some creative and innovative means to escape the confines of their prison perimeters. For example, inmates have used soap carved out to resemble a pistol with sun-baked black shoe polish to give it that finish look to successfully escape during transports with law enforcement personnel. Or inmates who go on a hunger strike to lose enough weight after greasing up their bodies with lotion or oil to slide through HVAC ductwork in an attempt to escape.

Well, Rocket Man was no exception, but his method is pretty unique and unusual. Rocket Man was a sex offender who typically would get beat up once or twice a week after other inmates learned of his gruesome crimes. Rocket Man couldn't stand it anymore and decided he had to get out of there. He was assigned to the maintenance department, which afforded him direct access to tools and materials to aid in his escape from the confines of the prison.

A maintenance supervisor just happened to catch Rocket Man constructing a saddle that he planned to use. His plan was to strap himself to a compressed gas cylinder and break off the head of the cylinder, which would propel him over the double razor-wired fences to freedom. Needless to say, his escape attempt had been foiled only to live another day in confinement. Staff and inmates now refer to him as the Rocket Man.

The Executive Who
Was Knee Deep in It

The director of a department of corrections took his executive team out to an acreage to review it for a potential site of a new prison. As the group unloaded off the bus and as they gathered around to view the site, the head of the maintenance and construction department decided to peel-off of the group and go take a closer look at the area and its perimeter. All of a sudden, it was noticed by another team member that the head of the maintenance and construction department was screaming and yelling, "HELP, HELP, HELP."

As he got other team members' attention, all noticed that he was sinking into the ground, not just any ground, but he was sinking in a sewer hole. The executive was almost waist deep in human manure until he was pulled out. The director and others got a big laugh out of the incident when one said they always knew he was full of it!

Boomerang Gas

During a major riot at a maximum security prison, correctional emergency squads were summoned from nearby correctional facilities to help quell the disturbance of rioting inmates. As each team received their assignments, they all took off in different directions to carry out their orders.

One team's mission was to apprehend and control a number of inmates that were positioned up against a brick wall near one corner of the yard compound. As the squad got in a V position to begin marching toward the inmates, with riot batons and shields in hand, it was decided by one squad member near the back of the group to use a gas grenade to disburse the group, making it easier to apprehend and control each individual inmate.

So as the squad got closer to the group of inmates, the squad member near the back launched a gas grenade landing in front of the group of inmates. About that time, the wind shifted, and the gas started to come back toward the squad and its members. All the squad members were ordered to stop and put on their gas masks as inmates fell to the ground in laughter. For a split moment, that event eased the stressful moment among staff and inmates.

The Squealing Inmate

An inmate housed at a medium security facility was found missing from the 4:30 p.m. inmate count. All inmates had to be accounted for prior to releasing them from their cells to go eat in the unit's dining hall for dinner.

During the count, it was determined the inmate was not in his cell. Officers began searching other areas of the unit, but to no avail. He was nowhere to be found on his unit, so the search expanded facility wide, and all areas were being searched for the missing inmate. Other inmates became disruptive, screaming and hollering because they wanted out of their cells to go eat dinner at their scheduled time.

It was feared by correctional staff that the inmate had successfully escaped from the confines of the interior perimeter of the facility. The facility shut down all operations to focus on finding the missing inmate and determining if he escaped from the prison or was still inside the facility grounds. Other areas of the prison did not go unnoticed, and staff was searching utility chases, the gymnasium, restrooms, offices, and even the chapel.

Suddenly, staff heard a loud squealing yell of someone screaming in an apparent state of agonizing pain. The sound grew louder and louder until it was observed by staff the unit captain had the missing inmate by the nap of his neck and was pulling upward the hair on the back of his head, which caused the inmate to walk on his tippy-toes. As the inmate was screaming and crying, the unit captain was giving him a piece of his mind. Needless to say, the inmate never tried that stunt again!

Other books by Dan Reynolds include:

The Most Hilarious, Bizarre and Unusual Correctional Stories Ever Told

On the Other Side of the Bars - Lessons Learned as a Prison Warden/Administrator

History of the Oklahoma State Penitentiary 1908 – 2015 (2nd edition)

Caged Wisdom: Learning to See through the Bars

The Riot of '73 - Oklahoma State Penitentiary

What God Wants You To Know

History of Oklahoma State Penitentiary Rodeo

These books are available wherever you like to buy books.

You may contact Dan Reynolds for speaking engagements, appearances or autographed book copies at dan1reynolds@yahoo.com

CPSIA information can be obtained
at www.ICGtesting.com
Printed in the USA
BVHW062212250122
627126BV00017B/794